# Dandelion Readers

4 in a Row Games practising the following:

1-  Alphabet sounds
2-  First vowel sounds
3-  CVC
4-  CVC with ff, ll, ss
5-  CVCC
6-  CCVC
7-  CCVCC
8-  'ch'
9-  'sh'
10- 'ch' and 'sh'
11- 'th'
12- 'ck'
13- 'ng'
14- Blank 4 in a Row

© Phonic Books Ltd. 2006
Enquiries@phonicbooks.co.uk
www.phonicbooks.co.uk

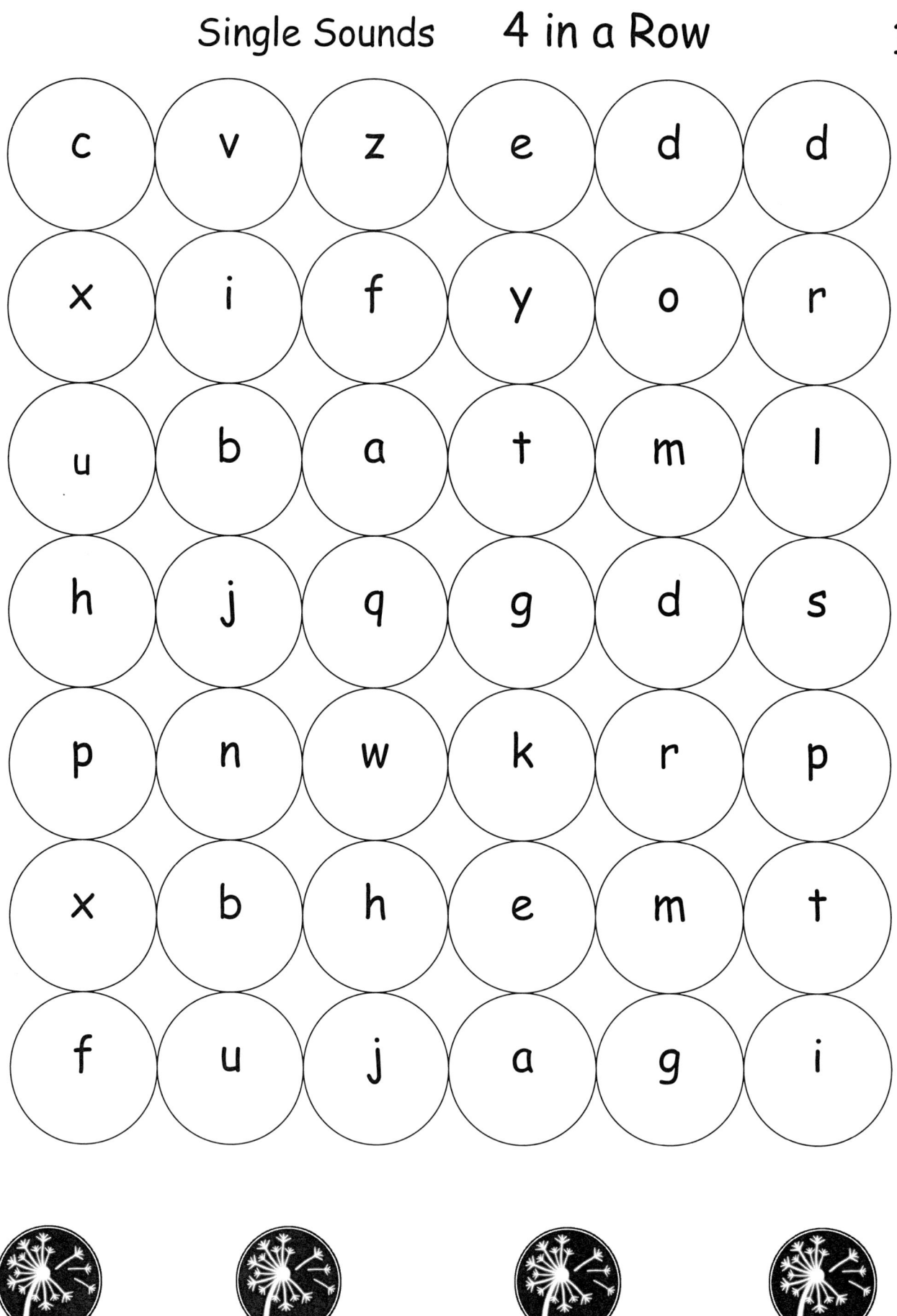

Two different sets of coloured counters are needed.  Two players take it in turns to say the sound and put a counter on the letter.  The winner is the first to get four counters in a row.
Play four games.  When a game is won the winner places a counter on a dandelion.

| a | i | e | o | u | i |
| e | o | u | i | a | o |
| u | e | i | a | e | u |
| o | a | u | o | i | a |
| i | e | i | a | u | e |
| a | o | a | e | i | o |
| u | i | u | o | u | e |

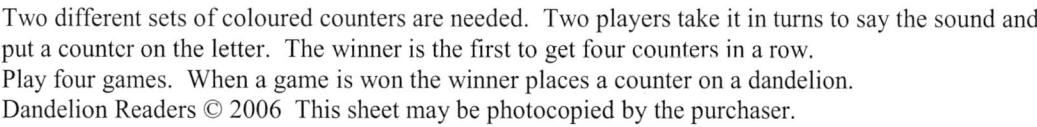

Two different sets of coloured counters are needed.  Two players take it in turns to say the sound and put a counter on the letter.  The winner is the first to get four counters in a row.
Play four games.  When a game is won the winner places a counter on a dandelion.
Dandelion Readers © 2006  This sheet may be photocopied by the purchaser.

| log | tap | sit | cub | pet |
| fun | get | job | dad | win |
| mum | big | lad | hug | bed |
| hit | jug | let | pot | man |
| nod | van | kit | mud | fed |
| hen | cup | top | mat | sit |
| sit | fat | red | rug | fog |

Two different sets of coloured counters are needed. Two players take it in turns to read the word and put a counter on the word. The winner is the first to get four counters in a row.

Play four games. When a game is won the winner places a counter on a dandelion.

| | | | | |
|---|---|---|---|---|
| cog | puff | sit | cab | less |
| fig | get | doll | dad | fun |
| mud | big | lass | dog | bell |
| fill | jog | set | pill | man |
| vet | van | kiss | mud | fill |
| fell | loss | rug | mat | sit |
| less | fat | bill | fun | doll |

Two different sets of coloured counters are needed.  Two players take it in turns to read the word and put a counter on the word.  The winner is the first to get four counters in a row.
Play four games.  When a game is won the winner places a counter on a dandelion.

Two different sets of coloured counters are needed.  Two players take it in turns to read the word and put a counter on the word.  The winner is the first to get four counters in a row.
Play four games.  When a game is won the winner places a counter on a dandelion.

| | | | | |
|---|---|---|---|---|
| slip | grab | crop | blot | twin |
| grin | swim | fret | stiff | dress |
| drab | flap | flop | drip | slug |
| spit | crab | grip | spill | grub |
| smell | trap | twig | drab | spell |
| snot | pram | stop | still | gruff |
| swam | slap | stuff | from | frill |

Two different sets of coloured counters are needed. Two players take it in turns to read the word and put a counter on the word. The winner is the first to get four counters in a row.
Play four games. When a game is won the winner places a counter on a dandelion.

| | | | | |
|---|---|---|---|---|
| drink | scamp | bland | spent | grand |
| twins | crest | glint | frisk | twist |
| stand | print | blink | skunk | slept |
| stump | scalp | craft | grunt | stamp |
| blond | trunk | blend | tramp | stank |
| blunt | slept | crisp | frost | brisk |

Two different sets of coloured counters are needed. Two players take it in turns to read the word and put a counter on the word. The winner is the first to get four counters in a row.
Play four games. When a game is won the winner places a counter on a dandelion.

| champ | such | inch | lunch | rich |
| chin | punch | chunk | chimp | chill |
| pinch | chap | chest | chum | chops |
| munch | chips | finch | bench | chess |
| chops | chimp | chat | such | chunk |
| chops | lunch | champ | pinch | chums |

Two different sets of coloured counters are needed. Two players take it in turns to read the word and put a counter on the word. The winner is the first to get four counters in a row.
Play four games. When a game is won the winner places a counter on a dandelion.
Dandelion Readers © 2006 This sheet may be photocopied by the purchaser.

| | | | | |
|---|---|---|---|---|
| shed | shin | shop | shall | shelf |
| shot | bash | brush | shell | shift |
| dish | shrub | fish | gash | shush |
| cash | rush | shift | wish | shelf |
| shred | ship | shed | fish | brush |
| brush | crash | shop | wish | shall |

Two different sets of coloured counters are needed. Two players take it in turns to read the word and put a counter on the word. The winner is the first to get four counters in a row.
Play four games. When a game is won the winner places a counter on a dandelion.
Dandelion Readers © 2006 This sheet may be photocopied by the purchaser.

| | | | | |
|---|---|---|---|---|
| shed | chimp | such | shall | shelf |
| lunch | bash | brush | shell | chops |
| munch | shrub | chest | gash | chunk |
| cash | chips | shift | rich | shelf |
| shred | chums | bench | fish | brush |
| pinch | crash | punch | wish | chest |

Two different sets of coloured counters are needed. Two players take it in turns to read the word and put a counter on the word. The winner is the first to get four counters in a row.
Play four games. When a game is won the winner places a counter on a dandelion.
Dandelion Readers © 2006 This sheet may be photocopied by the purchaser.

| | | | | |
|---|---|---|---|---|
| thank | thump | with | path | that |
| thud | moth | throb | broth | sixth |
| this | theft | cloth | think | thin |
| depth | fifth | thin | them | broth |
| think | thank | moth | sixth | throb |
| cloth | depth | them | that | bath |

Two different sets of coloured counters are needed.  Two players take it in turns to read the word and put a counter on the word.  The winner is the first to get four counters in a row.
Play four games.  When a game is won the winner places a counter on a dandelion.

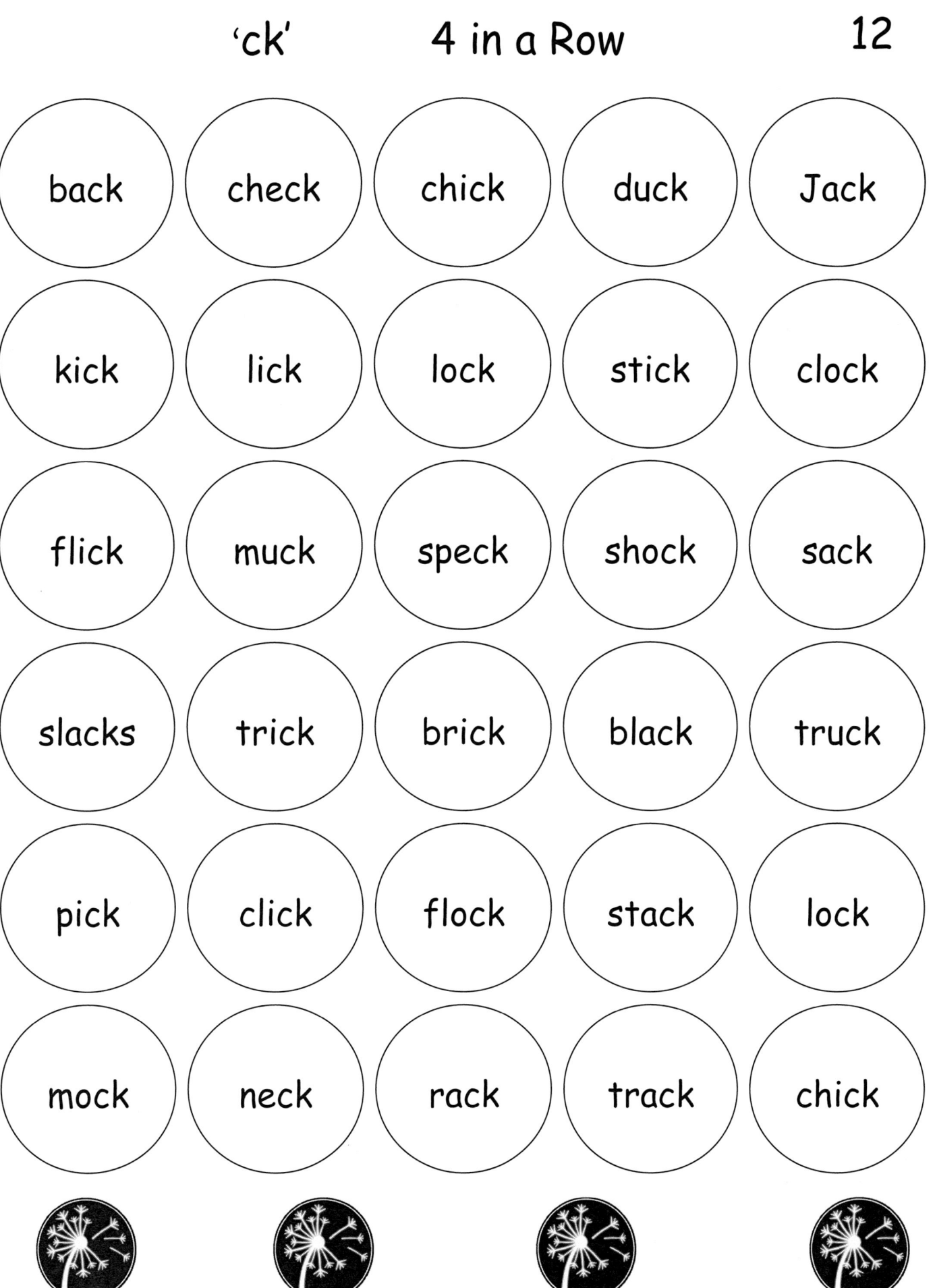

| | | | | |
|---|---|---|---|---|
| back | check | chick | duck | Jack |
| kick | lick | lock | stick | clock |
| flick | muck | speck | shock | sack |
| slacks | trick | brick | black | truck |
| pick | click | flock | stack | lock |
| mock | neck | rack | track | chick |

Two different sets of coloured counters are needed. Two players take it in turns to read the word and put a counter on the word. The winner is the first to get four counters in a row.
Play four games. When a game is won the winner places a counter on a dandelion.
Dandelion Readers © 2006 This sheet may be photocopied by the purchaser.

| bang | brings | clang | sting | song |
| cling | long | fling | king | lungs |
| prong | ring | slang | sung | sling |
| sing | stings | swing | thing | twang |
| wing | rang | bring | songs | king |
| fling | lungs | thing | ring | bang |

Two different sets of coloured counters are needed. Two players take it in turns to read the word and
put a counter on the word. The winner is the first to get four counters in a row.
Play four games. When a game is won the winner places a counter on a dandelion.

Two different sets of coloured counters are needed. Two players take it in turns to read the word and put a counter on the word. The winner is the first to get four counters in a row.
Play four games. When a game is won the winner places a counter on a dandelion.